FORT WORTH

Then & NOW

FORT WORTH

Then & NOW

Text by Carol Roark
Contemporary photographs by Rodger Mallison
Foreword by Douglas Harman

TCU PRESS • FORT WORTH

Library of Congress Cataloging-in-Publication Data

Roark, Carol E.
        Fort Worth then and now / text by Carol Roark ; contemporary photography by Rodger
Mallison ; forward by Douglas Harman.
        p. cm.
        Includes index.
        ISBN 0-87565-245-X (alk. paper)
        1. Fort Worth (Tex.)--History--Pictorial works. 2. Fort Worth (Tex.)--Pictorial works.
3. Fort Worth (Tex.)--History. I. Mallison, Rodger. II. Title.

F394.F7 R63 2001
976.4'5315--dc21

                                                                                      2001037034
                                                                                      Printed in Canada

Jacket/Book Design/Margie Adkins Graphic Design

DEDICATIONS

For Larry, who saw a beautiful world through the lens of his camera.
Carol Roark

To Tom Mallison and Gene Gordon: good men and good photographers
who walked this path before me and showed me the way.
Rodger Mallison

CONTENTS

Cities have long been fascinating subjects of study. Over the years, there have been many methods and approaches to the analysis of cities. The development of photography over a century and a half ago offered yet another way that cities could be examined. In some respects, examination of the city through photography is unbiased. Yet all photography inherently creates bias by what is and is not photographed and by the limitations of the camera. Ultimately, therefore, urban photographs create opportunities for individuals to study the images and to reach judgments and observations on their own. This is especially the case when cities are photographed over time. *Fort Worth Then & Now* is a strong example of the study of a city through the lens of cameras over years of time.

Fort Worth is an unusually appropriate city for this type of time study because it has long been a community with a special feeling about its past and about its development. It is a city that prides itself on historic preservation and on strong commitment to "good" urban development. *Fort Worth Then & Now* is an in-depth review of this community, but conclusions about the city are really left to each individual who studies the comparative photographs. Without a doubt, remarkable examples of city preservation can be seen in these photographs. Unfortunately, there are also examples of significant attractive areas that no longer exist. Some areas of the early city were never caught by the camera's lens, so no comparative photographs can be produced today.

Fort Worth Then & Now is a strong contribution to urban studies and should be of great interest to many different audiences. Everyone interested in urban preservation will find this book as an excellent example of how a single community can be studied through comparative photography. It is also a case study of an important Texas city with deep frontier and western roots. As seen in these photographs, Fort Worth saved much of its stockyards area. It is one of the only major livestock centers in the United States to have done so. Today the Fort Worth Stockyards National Historic District is a great example of the possibilities in converting obsolete industrial and agricultural areas into a tourism districts.

Readers familiar with Fort Worth will want to compare the old and new photographs carefully, looking for the details of change over time. Those not so familiar with this city should also gain much from this city analysis because the technique is easily applicable to other cities having early photographic records. Clearly the study of Fort Worth will need to be updated in future years. Major urban development plans now underway will necessitate future photographic review and comparison.

We can be thankful that the invention of the camera many years ago made this study possible and allowed us all to enjoy the evolution of our city over time from the perspectives of the lens and interpretation by various individuals. In taking the contemporary photographs, Rodger Mallison has been scrupulously careful to adopt the position and viewpoint of the photographer of the original image.

Douglas Harman
Fort Worth Convention & Visitors Bureau
May 2001

ACKNOWLEDGMENTS

Research is a bit like assembling a puzzle. Sometimes the piece doesn't seem to fit anywhere, until you get to a point in the project where its place is suddenly apparent. At other times, the researcher searches for a particular piece and finds it only with the aid of others who are not actually working on the puzzle. This project, in particular, has been an assemblage, starting with the hunt for suitable historic photographs. The staff of local institutions and several private collectors have been very helpful in this process. In particular, I would like to thank the Special Collections staff at the University of Texas at Arlington—Sally Gross, Ann Hodges, Kit Goodwin, Gary Spurr, and Donita Maligi—for their help in mining the *Fort Worth Star-Telegram* files and other collections. Tom Kellam, Max Hill, Shirley Apley, and Ken Hopkins at the Fort Worth Public Library also provided valuable assistance. Doug Jones, Records Manager for the City of Fort Worth, generously offered the use of photographs recently discovered in the course of processing the city's archival holdings, and Steven L. Fenberg, Community Affairs Coordinator with the Houston Endowment Inc., generously opened his collection concerning Jesse H. Jones' business interests for me. Private collectors still hold many wonderful Fort Worth images not found in institutional collections, and I am grateful to Quentin McGown, IV, Dalton Hoffman, Larry Schuessler, and Brian Perkins who were each eager to share their treasures.

Other individuals helped me identify or date photographs, and without their assistance this book would be incomplete. Any errors are, of course, my responsibility, but I am grateful to Jim Noah, Evelyn Riscky Logan, Ruby Schmidt, Frank Moss, Jimm Foster, Andy Reisberg, and the staff of Pendery's World of Chiles & Spices for sharing their knowledge about particular photographs.

Collaborating with Rodger Mallison on this project has been enjoyable. He had been taking "then & now" shots of Fort Worth before work on the book began, and his passion for the project was unmistakable. Rodger has a keen eye and a wicked sense of humor, both of which contributed greatly to the success of this endeavor. Judy Alter, the director of TCU Press is both a friend and a colleague, and I respect and appreciate the guidance she gave in shaping the text of this volume. I also want to thank my family, especially my husband, Lon, and sister, Linda, for helping me juggle this project among several others while keeping the home fires burning.

Carol Roark
May 2001

Thanks to Carol Roark, my partner in this endeavor. Her organizational skills—the stock and trade of archivists—are vital for a project like this. But, more important, her love for Fort Worth and her passion for its history inspired and instructed me. I was never able to think of a question she could not answer in detail and with all the wonderful little nuances that make history fun. Cheers to Margie Adkins West, a great designer, who doesn't get enough credit because her wonderful clean designs let the words and photos speak. Special thanks to Jeffery Washington and Sharon Corcoran who loaned me cameras to use. You saved me. And thanks to all the building supervisors who let me on their buildings or helped me ponder which window to photograph from. They were a wealth of help and information—and great fun to visit with.

Rodger Mallison
June 2001

INTRODUCTION

Fort Worth: Then & Now

Fort Worth fits many longtime residents like a comfortable shoe. We know the best shortcuts to our favorite spots, where the best views are, and what to show out-of-town visitors to make a good impression. Although we may be aware of the changes taking place around us, our sense of place—the way we remember the city, the streets, the buildings, and the people—is complex. Our memory preserves the Fort Worth of times past and incorporates those impressions and experiences into our understanding of the Fort Worth today.

Change and the Landscape

Some aspects of the landscape seem immutable. Rivers and hills don't appear to change—or to change only at a glacial pace as a result of the forces of nature. If asked, most Fort Worth residents would tell you that the Trinity River bluff where the fort was sited and courthouse now stands probably looks substantially the same today as it did when the fort was active in the late 1840s. We have no photographs from the earliest years, but turn-of-the-century images show that while the features of the bridges crossing the Trinity have changed, the general shape of the bluff endures.

In some cases humans have, in fact, changed the land itself. Sections of the Trinity River have been dammed and channeled, taming a stream that once periodically sent floodwaters raging through the city. Today the Trinity, where it runs through Fort Worth, is—for better or worse—a managed urban river. Its banks are no longer steep and covered with brambles but manicured and often flanked with hiking and biking trails. Yet, most people alive today remember only the controlled Trinity and don't have a sense of the human effort that went into shaping its course.

We do expect some change from man-made features of the landscape. Major construction projects like dams and highways drastically alter the shape of the landscape. Once built, however, they seem almost eternal to those who live with them day by day. Constructed in 1914, the Lake Worth Dam now has the patina of age. Inspiration Point offered a view of the dam and a lake that reflected moonlight for young lovers in 1940, and under the light of the next full moon it will present that view again.

Change in the city streetscape is an amalgam. With the exception of major landmarks—the courthouse, Livestock Exchange, or Flatiron Building, for example—our sense of a streetscape is a collage of the various elements: buildings, roadway, streetlights, plantings, and activity patterns. Change only one piece, and our perception of the streetscape remains much the same. Who has not driven down a road a year after a new building had replaced an old one and had trouble remembering exactly what the old structure looked like? The scene seems much the same to us overall, and only with concentration can we pick out the changes. Yet, if we change too many of the pieces at once—wipe out a row of buildings, widen the roadway, or change the lighting and street furniture we are forced to develop a new reaction to the scene whether we like the changes or not. Our old understanding of the landscape is relegated to our memory banks because it is no longer useful for daily life.

A Sense of Place

Even when it is not needed for daily activities, the memory of a place is powerful. Our mind holds pictures of the places we have frequented over the years, forming a rich tapestry of sense, experience, and associative memory. This sense of place blends the physical features of the landscape we have lived in with our experiences in it. We may associate a certain place with a significant event or perhaps the familiarity comes from repeated visits. Fort Worth's downtown streets are no longer lined with major department stores, yet many people walking downtown look at the historic buildings and remember shopping at The Fair or having lunch in Monnig's tearoom. That experience is a rich part of their sense of place.

The physical characteristics of a place contribute to what we remember about it. A building may be particularly attractive; possessing architectural features or details that we appreciate. Or, like the Knights of Pythias Castle Hall, it may be unique—something so unusual that it leaves a lasting impression. Those features become part of our mental files, to be recalled when we see something that reminds us of the structure or are asked to describe it.

Patterns of use also influence our sense of place. The road we drove to get to summer camp, or work, or school stays in our memory. At times, we may not be aware of our actions as we automatically curve at each curve, stop at each stop sign, and tick off the buildings we pass. Years later, when the road has been straightened and only a few of the buildings remain, we can almost play a mental tape of the old landscape as we drive through the new one.

Several years ago, I stood with my father in the lobby of the Texas & Pacific Railway Terminal Building as he told stories about traveling to Fort Worth by train while he was in the military. In his mind, the station was full of people waiting to greet their loved ones, and his mother and father were at the front of the crowd watching expectantly for his appearance. The grand lobby space of the T&P was an impressive setting for a homesick young soldier meeting his family. Merely seeing the space years later triggered strong memories of that important moment and the impact that the grand space had on him.

Then & Now

This collection of Fort Worth photographs gives us an opportunity to examine images made over more than a century of the city's history and compare them with our own experience. Some, such as the 1883-1884 view of Main Street, show a scene that no one alive today has seen. Our sense of the historic appearance of the Sundance Square area comes from reading the historical markers or promotional materials. It is interesting to compare the historic photograph not only to the street scene as it appears today but to our mental image of what Sundance Square must have looked like almost 120 years ago.

In Fort Worth, the twentieth-century landscape contains more points of reference for most viewers. Only isolated aspects of the nineteenth-century landscape remain—a building here, a monument there—and people may have a difficult time reconciling that one piece with the drastically altered contemporary scene. Photographs taken during the early years of the twentieth century may share enough elements with their contemporary counterparts that the scene is more easily recognized. Even though the businesses have changed, the current view of the intersection of Hemphill and Magnolia looks much the same today as it did sixty years ago. The small parking lot on the east side of the Paris Coffee Shop functions much as it did for the Safeway store. The traffic patterns, too, are similar, and Fort Worth National Bank, housed in the old Modern Drug store, has been recently renovated using historic photographs much like the one reproduced in this volume to restore much of its historic appearance.

In other photographs—the views along Camp Bowie Boulevard or East Lancaster looking towards downtown, for example—the distinctive shape of the roadway and the fact that the buildings flanking it maintain a similar scale and setback in both the historic and contemporary photographs allows us to match these scenes. In the pair of Camp Bowie Boulevard photographs, a single distinctive landmark—the Arlington Heights Masonic Lodge—provides a unique visual match point for both images. Although the building is not unusual in and of itself, it is set at an angle to Camp Bowie and so catches our eye as we scan the photographs.

Other comparisons may be based as much on how we perceived a particular event—the stock show parade or midway, for example—as on its similarity to the way the event appears today. The horses and carnival barkers are cues that allow anyone who has experienced the event to develop their own comparisons. People who haven't attended a stock show in Fort Worth may have a more objective analysis of each of these pairs of photographs than someone with a bank of historic memories, but each is valid.

Enjoy this opportunity to walk back in time through Fort Worth's history. Match the "reality" of the historic photographs with your own memory or expectations and compare it with the contemporary photographs, which stand in their own right as a compelling record of Fort Worth in 2001. There is a rich treasure of memory and change to be explored.

Carol Roark
May 2001

Downtown

Main Street
circa 1883-1884

Many Fort Worth residents think that today's Sundance Square area looks much the same as it did during the nineteenth century. This historic photograph, taken about 1883-1884, shows no buildings that are standing today. The Tarrant County Courthouse in the historic picture has been replaced by a building that was constructed in 1893-1895. Main Street was then dirt, not brick, and tracks for a horse-drawn streetcar ran down the middle of the roadway. The historic photograph does have one link with contemporary Fort Worth aside from location. The building closest to the viewer on the right is Temple Place, a grocery run by brothers Frank P., DeWitt C., and Eugene C. Pendery. Family sources say that DeWitt C. Pendery came to Fort Worth in 1870, six years before the railroad arrived, and his brother Frank soon joined him. They started in the wholesale liquor business, but soon became grocers and were joined by Eugene, the third brother. By the early 1890s, the brothers had gone into separate businesses, with DeWitt Pendery founding a company called Mexican Chile Supply Company. That company is still in business today, owned by Pendery descendents.

Flatiron Building
circa 1912

One of Fort Worth's most distinctive and beloved landmarks, the Flatiron Building has graced the city skyline since 1907. This building—and other similar buildings—are named for their wedge-shaped footprint. The form reminded many of the shape of the heavy metal irons once heated on a stove and then used to press clothes. At seven stories tall, the Flatiron may not look like a skyscraper to modern eyes but fits the definition for skyscrapers because it has a reinforced steel frame and uses an elevator to move people and goods to the top floors. The Flatiron was built by a physician, Dr. Bacon Saunders, and housed medical offices. Today, it is once again owned by a physician and is being renovated for commercial and residential use.

Historic photograph courtesy Fort Worth Public Library

5

Knights of Pythias Castle Hall
1910s

This building is one of Fort Worth's most distinctive landmarks. Generations have passed along fond memories of the knight in the niche (now a reproduction and not seen in either photograph) and pointed out the unusual structure to visiting friends and relatives. The hall, built to resemble a medieval guildhall, was erected for the Knights of Pythias, a fraternal society. Like many organizations that practiced rituals not shared outside the membership, the Knights built a multi-story building with commercial lease space on the ground and club facilities above—so the rituals could be conducted out of the view of passing strangers. Restored in 1983 as part of the Sundance Square redevelopment, the hall remains a Fort Worth favorite.

Texas State Bank
circa 1917-1918

The Texas State Bank, Carnegie Library, and Flatiron Building (just to the left out of the picture) helped make the intersection of 9th and Houston streets a busy place at the time of the First World War. The bank, built in 1906 by W. H. Eddleman—owner of the Ball-Eddleman-McFarland House—as the Western National Bank, now houses one of Fort Worth's many loft residential projects. The top two floors were added in 1918. The Carnegie Library, seen on the left in the historic photograph, was replaced by another library building in 1937, and the land is now used as a parking lot.

Historic photograph courtesy Special Collections, University of Texas at Arlington Libraries

Construction of
Paddock Viaduct
looking north, 1913-1914

Historic photograph courtesy Fort Worth Public Library

Although Fort Worth's site on a bluff overlooking the Trinity River was generally advantageous, the lack of ready access to the stockyards and other commercial and residential development north of the river was a drawback. Initially, ferries and low water crossings provided the only access across the Trinity at this point. Paddock Viaduct, the second bridge leading from the bluff to the north side, was constructed in 1913-1914, replacing an outmoded two-lane suspension bridge erected during the 1890s. The bridge was named for Buckley Boardman Paddock, a Fort Worth mayor, editor of the *Fort Worth Democrat* newspaper, and state legislator. A handsome example of municipal design, the bridge was named a Texas Historic Civil Engineering Landmark because it was the first reinforced concrete arch bridge in the nation to use self-supporting reinforcing steel. Comparing the historic and modern photographs, two significant changes are evident: the alteration of the concrete bridge railings, which were replaced by metal rails in 1964-1965, and alterations at the Fort Worth Power and Light/TXU facility in the background.

Mount Gilead Baptist Church
circa 1913

Motorists entering downtown Fort Worth from the east on either Fourth or Sixth streets pass a landmark that anchored the neighborhood around it for many decades. Mount Gilead Baptist Church was founded in 1875 and is considered the "mother church" of Fort Worth's African-American Baptist congregations. This building, constructed in 1912-1913, was an essential center for people whose skin color denied them access to basic services. The church offered child care, a swimming pool, a library, and a gymnasium as well as the more typical educational programs. When it was built, the church was at the heart of a vibrant African-American neighborhood that has since been replaced by commercial development. Although the houses around the church have disappeared and the surrounding commercial structures now dwarf it, Mount Gilead remains an icon to the community it serves

Historic photograph courtesy Fort Worth Public Library

13

Texas & Pacific Railway Terminal
with Al Hayne monument in the foreground, 1902

Historic photograph courtesy *Fort Worth Star-Telegram*

The Texas Spring Palace, built in 1889, was a massive wooden exhibit hall decorated inside and out with wheat, corn, cotton, and native grasses. The highly flammable structure burned on May 30, 1890, the closing night of the second season. Although the hall was crowded, only one person lost his life in the blaze. Alfred S. Hayne, who returned several times to rescue people from the building, died the next day from burns he suffered during his rescue attempts. In 1893, the Women's Humane Association dedicated a monument, which contained a watering fountain for horses, to Hayne near the site of the Spring Palace. It can be seen in both of these photographs. The 1902 image shows a crowd of West Texans, who were visiting Fort Worth, gathered around the monument, which sits in the middle of a large bricked plaza next to the Texas & Pacific Railway Terminal.

Today, the Hayne monument is the only surviving feature from the historic landscape. It sits, surrounded by construction on Lancaster Avenue and Interstate 30, on a landscaped triangle built in the early 1930s in conjunction with a bridge and street improvement program.

Carnegie
Public Library
circa 1905-1906

Fort Worth
Public Library
circa 1940

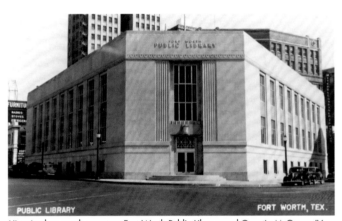

Historic photographs courtesy Fort Worth Public Library and Quentin McGown, IV

This corner site served as the location for Fort Worth's public library from 1901 until 1978. Conveniently located near the city hall, the library provided important information resources at a time when chain bookstores and the Internet were not available. The Carnegie Library—the city's first—opened on this site it 1901 on land donated by Sarah Gray Jennings. It was replaced by the Moderne structure in the center photograph in 1938. In the mid-1970s, the city decided to build a new central library adjacent to Tandy Center and turn the old library building over to other city departments. A clause in the donor's will specified, however, that if the land was not used for library purposes it would revert to the her heirs. The heirs reclaimed the property in 1980 and sold it to a developer who demolished the building in 1990, unable to find an alternative use for it. Today, the space is merely one among a number of downtown parking lots.

Looking west on Seventh Street
circa 1926

The historic photograph, taken looking west on Seventh Street, shows the Elks Club building on the right, and Burnett Park and the Medical Arts Building under construction on the left. Cattle baron Samuel Burk Burnett deeded land for the park to the City of Fort Worth in June 1919 with the stipulation that it always be used for park purposes. Burnett hired noted park planner George Kessler to design a master plan and willed $50,000 to the city for improvement of the land. No work was done until 1925, after both Burnett and Kessler had died, so the historic photograph shows the park's early design. Over the years, Burnett Park was a resting place for tired shoppers and business people as well as the home of the city's annual Christmas tree display. Developer Jesse H. Jones of Houston built the Medical Arts Building, located on the western edge of the park and completed in 1927, to

Historic photograph courtesy *Fort Worth Star-Telegram*

house medical offices. Because the medical district developed south of downtown, and there was limited parking at a time when automobile use was growing rapidly, the Medical Arts Building never reached its full potential. It was demolished on July 1, 1973. Burnett Park was completely renovated in 1984 with funding from the Anne Burnett and Charles Tandy Foundation.

West Seventh Street
looking east
circa 1930

West Seventh Street has long been one of the primary thoroughfares into the heart of Fort Worth's central business district. Two of the office towers in the historic photograph, the Electric and Neil P. Anderson buildings, still flank Seventh Street at Lamar. Against the backdrop of other downtown buildings, they look less like skyscrapers today than they did seventy years ago. The small building in the triangle-shaped piece of land in the historic picture is a Texas Pacific Coal & Oil Co. filling station, one of eight company stations in the Fort Worth area. The lot behind it is almost empty in the 1930 photograph, but today holds the One Burnett Plaza building which houses the Bank of America. The Bank One Tower, sheathed in plywood on the left side of the current photograph, is a relic of the 2000 Fort Worth tornado and was scheduled for demolition shortly after this picture was taken.

21

Majestic Theatre
1913

Historic photograph courtesy Special Collections, University of Texas at Arlington Libraries

Vaudeville began in the 1880s as family entertainment, contrasted with the more adult-oriented burlesque shows. The live shows provided light entertainment acts that drew their humor from everyday modern life. The most successful vaudeville houses were part of theater circuits. The Majestic, located at 1101 Commerce Street, was part of the premier "Orpheum Circuit," which also included theaters in San Francisco, Kansas City, Denver, Chicago, Dallas, and other cities. As motion pictures became popular, many vaudeville houses incorporated them into their program. Eventually, many former vaudeville venues, including the Majestic, became motion picture theaters. Martin Luther King, Jr., spoke at the Majestic on a visit to Fort Worth in October 1959. The Majestic was demolished in 1966 to make way for the Tarrant County Convention Center, and today the center's climate control equipment occupies the site.

Worth Theater and Hotel
circa 1932

The Worth Theater and Hotel complex was one of several downtown Fort Worth properties developed by Houston financier Jesse H. Jones. Located on Seventh Street behind the Fort Worth Club Building, the Worth Theater was one of three movie palaces, with the Hollywood and the Palace, along Fort Worth's "show row." Today, only an interior section of the Hollywood Theater remains, used as a parking garage for the Electric Building lofts. In their glory days, the theaters competed vigorously for patrons, and street displays such as this one for *Hell Divers*—a sentimental 1932 story of the rivalry between two Navy pilots starring Wallace Beery and Clark Gable—were common. The Fort Worth Club demolished the building in 1972 to build the Fort Worth Club Tower.

Historic photograph courtesy Dalton Hoffman

Ball-Eddleman-McFarland House
circa 1900

Recognized from Summit Avenue or the Lancaster Avenue Bridge by its picturesque roofline, the Ball-Eddleman-McFarland House is one of Fort Worth's most significant Victorian-era landmarks. In an age well before the development of air-conditioning, the builders sited this Queen Anne mansion on a bluff overlooking the Trinity River to capture the breezes. The house was completed in 1898-1899 for the wealthy Galveston widow Sarah C. Ball and her son Frank. It is best known, however, as the home of Caroline Eddleman McFarland, who moved into the house with her parents and cattleman husband, Frank Hays McFarland, in 1904 and lived here until her death in 1978. Mrs. McFarland's tenacity preserved this jewel for generations to come when other Quality Hill landmarks were being demolished to "make way for progress."

Historic photograph courtesy Fort Worth Public Library

Fort Worth Star-Telegram mailroom

Historic photograph courtesy Special Collections, University of Texas at Arlington Libraries

Automation has made it possible to do larger jobs with fewer people, but even in highly mechanized operations humans play a necessary role. The primary contrast between these photographs of *Fort Worth Star-Telegram* mailroom operations is one of scale. In the historic image, the piles of paper and people are similar in size—but the large towering pallets of newspapers in today's mailroom can be moved only with machinery. Although there are about the same number of workers in both photographs, the scale of the operation in the historic image is dwarfed by the cavernous warehouse housing the current *Star-Telegram* mailroom. Yet, the current mailroom still requires people to direct the machines' output.

29

Fire Station No. 1
circa 1908

Fire Station No. 1
circa 1974-75

Historic photographs courtesy Special Collections,
University of Texas at Arlington Libraries

Buildings—even those built for a specific purpose—can be adapted for uses other than those originally intended. Fire Station No. 1 was built in 1907 on the site of Fort Worth's first city hall. The station served the central business district at a time when horse-drawn fire wagons were the norm. It originally had a back door and the southeast corner was "clipped" at an angle to allow horses to pull the equipment into the station rather than backing it in. After September 1919, when motorized equipment completely replaced horse-drawn wagons in Fort Worth fire stations, the old stable area in back was converted to a kitchen. Over time fire engines grew larger, but even as late as the 1970s the front opening could still accommodate one careful driver with a truck. The old station was abandoned by the Fire Department in 1980, and in 1983 it was renovated as part of the Sundance Square project to house a Fort Worth history exhibit developed by the Fort Worth Museum of Science and History.

31

Downtown skyline from the west side of the Trinity River
circa 1966-67

Skylines define a city in a way that no other view can, and photographers have long chronicled development by taking skyline pictures from the same point of view over time. The lay of the land in these images, shot from Trinity Park looking east across the Trinity River, seems to have changed little over the years. Yet, the views are very different when examined closely. Nature is more closely "managed" in the contemporary photograph—with paved paths, a gentler slope to the river, and turf that is mowed and edged. The skyline has changed as well. The courthouse, a dominant building on the left side of the historical image, is dwarfed in comparison with the skyscrapers in the photograph shot in 2001.

Belknap Street Bridge
1933

Historic photograph courtesy *Fort Worth Star-Telegram*

Both of these photographs show construction on the Belknap Street Bridge at the northeast corner of the central business district. The historic bridge was sometimes called the Belknap Street Overpass because it carried traffic over the Chicago, Rock Island & Gulf Railway (now Burlington Northern Santa Fe) tracks between downtown and the Riverside neighborhood. The historic 1210 foot bridge, with its graceful parabolic arch, was completed in 1933 at a cost of $350,000. Sixty-seven years later, workers demolished the historic bridge and built a new one in its place.

Looking east on West Lancaster Avenue from Jennings, Post Office on right
early 1930s

Historic photograph courtesy *Fort Worth Star-Telegram*

Lancaster Avenue, named in honor of former Texas & Pacific Railway president John L. Lancaster, forms the southern boundary of Fort Worth's central business district. The historic photograph shows the recently completed United States Post Office on the right. It is much grander in terms of both scale and design than the warehouses on the north side of the street. The Post Office was built close to the T&P tracks, which run along the backside of the building, to facilitate mail transport by rail. The warehouses, too, were located near rail services and served by a short spur that ran down Lancaster directly in front of the buildings. Thus the historic photograph speaks to the importance of railroads even though automobiles seem to dominate the image, while the dominating presence of the soon-to-be-demolished overhead freeway in the contemporary photograph demonstrates the impact of the automobile even though there are fewer vehicles visible in the historic picture.

37

Texas & Pacific Railway Terminal lobby
circa 1931

Historic photograph courtesy Special Collections, University of Texas at Arlington Libraries

The Texas & Pacific Railway Terminal's grand lobby dates to a time when travel was more of an adventure than an obligation and majestic entryways set the tone as travelers arrived at their destination. The magnificent Zigzag Moderne terminal was completed in 1931, just as Fort Worth and the rest of the nation was sliding into the depths of the Great Depression. Still, it bustled as a transportation hub, and many families have memories of greeting friends and relatives—or bidding them goodbye—in this opulent hall. Today, the recently restored lobby once again shines as the former depot is poised to host both Amtrak and commuter rail traffic. Plans call for the concourse and the office tower above the lobby to be converted for hotel use.

39

Intersection of Jennings and Lancaster avenues looking north
1931

Most people familiar with Fort Worth's Lancaster Avenue before the overhead freeway was built recall a street that was more human in scale and flanked with buildings that are local architectural landmarks. Yet, historic photographs of this gateway boulevard show an odd mix of pleasing urban design and gritty commercial practicality. This 1931 view is not so much a picturesque parkway as an urban street that allows people to move from one task to another. But it does have a more human sense of scale than the contemporary photograph. The back of St. Patrick's Cathedral is visible in both photos.

The elevated section of Interstate 30 dominates the contemporary photograph. A relic of Fort Worth's adaptation to the highway age, it is now scheduled for demolition

41

Frank Kent Ford,
Lancaster Avenue,
and Al Hayne triangle
from the T&P
Terminal
circa 1950

Highway systems are thoroughfares that allow us to speed through cities, but their construction has a major impact on the urban landscape. This historic photograph shows Frank Kent's well-known automobile dealership at the corner of Main and Lancaster and the stretch of Lancaster Avenue on the eastern edge of the central business district. Kent was a Ford dealer until 1953, when he was offered a Cadillac franchise. This view from atop the Texas & Pacific Terminal shows the many warehouse facilities that bordered downtown offices. The elevated freeway, which opened to traffic early in 1960, forever changed Lancaster. Remnants of the overhead are visible at the left edge of the contemporary photograph, now dwarfed by the broad curve of the new segment of Interstate 30 that defines the photograph. The Al Hayne triangle, with its monument to the man killed in the 1890 Spring Palace fire, is one of the few surviving pieces in both photographs.

Houston Street looking north from Eleventh Street
circa 1926

This foreground of this view of Houston Street shows a small northwestern section of the old Hell's Half Acre area, demolished in the 1960s to build the Tarrant County Convention Center. By the time the historic photograph was taken in the mid-1920s, the Acre was a mere shadow of its former self. The skyscraper on the left is the W. T. Waggoner Building, built by the oil baron and cattle king for whom the building was named and completed in 1919-1920. Today it is almost hidden among the taller buildings in the Fort Worth skyline. The twenty-four story Farmers and Mechanics National Bank Building, the tallest building on the right side of the street in the historic photograph, and behind the TXU Electric & Gas Building in the contemporary photograph, holds its place in the skyline better than the Waggoner Building, even though it is only four stories taller.

Electric Building
from Burnett Park
circa 1930

The Electric Service Company Building, known to most simply as the Electric Building, was erected in 1929-1930 for Houston developer and civic leader Jesse H. Jones. Designed by local architect Wyatt C. Hedrick, it housed the Texas Electric Service Company in the main tower and the Hollywood Theatre in the six-story annex located just to the north. Both the Electric Building and its neighbor to the south, the Neil P. Anderson Building, are Fort Worth preservation success stories. The Anderson Building, which housed many cotton and grain companies and had a cotton showroom and grading facility on the eleventh floor, was renovated for office use and the exterior restored to its historic appearance in 1977, making it one of Fort Worth's first commercial historic preservation projects. In 1968, the Houston Endowment Inc., which oversees Jones' business interests, donated the Electric Building to Texas Wesleyan College. It was subsequently sold several times and the interior insensitively remodeled. Finally, in 1996, the building was renovated for use as loft apartments by The Alexander Company. Today, the buildings proudly flank the Seventh Street gateway into downtown Fort Worth.

Historic photograph courtesy the Houston Endowment Inc.

Stock Show Parade on Main Street
March 12, 1937

For more than a century, the stock show parade has been a major annual event in Fort Worth. Billed as the world's largest all-western, non-motorized parade, the event gives cowboys and cowgirls—both real and pretend—the opportunity to show off their horses and western finery. The event solidifies the image of the West that has become a focal point in defining Fort Worth's character. The stock show and parade shifted from a March date to the latter part of January in 1948 to facilitate the establishment of a circuit of stock shows. In 1937, the parade shared Main Street with a streetcar headed for the Polytechnic Heights neighborhood. That may be the only significant difference, however, as the pageantry in the 2001 parade has a decidedly traditional feel.

Historic photograph courtesy Special Collections, University of Texas at Arlington Libraries

First Methodist Church
circa 1931

Historic photograph courtesy Special Collections, University of Texas at Arlington Libraries

Churches have long been important neighborhood anchors. When the neighborhood around them changes, many find it difficult to thrive. They often move, following their congregations. In 1931, the First Methodist Episcopal Church South locked the doors of its old building at Seventh and Taylor, where there was increasing commercial development, and moved a few blocks north and west to this new and much larger structure. The church's new neighborhood was still largely residential as this historic photograph shows. John Peter Smith School, the large brick building just north of the church, is the only other non-residential structure in the immediate vicinity. Today, almost all of the houses and small apartment buildings that once surrounded the church have been demolished and replaced either by parking lots or commercial development. This time, however, the church has chosen to stay. First Methodist now draws its congregation from throughout Fort Worth and Tarrant County, aided by its relative proximity to a freeway and ample free parking.

Looking west on Lancaster Avenue Texas & Pacific Warehouse
March 10, 1952

West Lancaster Avenue in 1952 was an area on the brink of a long downhill slide. Plans for construction of the downtown segment of the east-west freeway along Lancaster had just been announced, and the proposed route was mired in controversy. Railroad freight businesses housed in the Texas & Pacific Warehouse were losing ground to the trucking industry, and many small businesses along the north side of Lancaster were closing as passenger rail traffic declined. The Post Office Drug Store, seen in the right foreground, was one of the casualties. Eventually, the overhead freeway would cut the buildings on the south side of Lancaster off from the rest of downtown. For several decades business was conducted in the shadow of the overhead but the area did not prosper. The contemporary photograph seems even more desolate because of the lack of human scale. Today, the area is poised for rebirth when the overhead freeway is demolished. A landscaped boulevard could return not only the human scale of the district but also give it an ambiance it has lacked for far too long.

53

Looking north on Main Street
1942

In 1942, the nationally known photographer Arthur Rothstein traveled through the Fort Worth-Dallas area taking documentary photographs for the United States government. The project, which was begun during the Great Depression, shifted focus when World War II began, and most of Rothstein's images are of defense efforts at the "bomber plant" and Meacham Field rather than the more typical Farm Security Administration photographs that chronicled everyday life in America. This is the only view Rothstein made of downtown Fort Worth. It evokes a strong sense of nostalgia, not only because of the period buildings like the Bowen Bus line terminal and the Monnig's Warehouse (now Water Garden Place), but also for the more human sense of scale missing in the contemporary photograph.

Historic photograph courtesy Prints & Photographs Division, Library of Congress

Texas Street, looking west from Burnett
1953

Historic photograph courtesy Dalton Hoffman

As late as the 1950s, there were still a significant number of houses in downtown Fort Worth. Their numbers were dwindling as nineteenth-century residents—who built homes on the edge of a much smaller central business district—died and the properties were converted to commercial use. The resident of the charming, tree-shaded house on the right in the historic photograph was Mary Nixon, a widow. She had lived to see many changes in her neighborhood. Fort Worth's Art Deco Central Fire Station, built just down and across the street in 1930, still provides fire protection services. The Burnett Arms, not one of Fort Worth's premiere hostelries, is now a parking lot.

Throckmorton Street looking south from Fifth Street
circa 1945-1948

Downtown Fort Worth was thriving when this bustling historic photograph of Throckmorton Street was made shortly after World War II. According to a U.S. Census of Business for 1948, Fort Worth ranked seventh nationwide in per capita retail sales among cities with a population between 250,000 and 500,000 people and thirty-sixth nationwide in total volume of retail sales. Many people from nearby small cities and towns came to Fort Worth to shop. In 1946, for example, 21,899 out-of-towners had charge accounts at one of Fort Worth's eleven major department stores (including The Fair shown here). Today, major retail activity has shifted away from downtown to shopping malls, but the central business district is still economically viable. A mix of office, residential, and entertainment uses draws people to the downtown area giving new uses to its strong collection of historic buildings—including the Texas & Pacific Terminal, Petroleum, Fort Worth Club, and Fair buildings seen in these photographs.

Historic photograph courtesy the Houston Endowment Inc.

59

Tarrant County Convention Center and remnants of the old Hell's Half Acre
circa 1970

Historic photograph courtesy Quentin McGown, IV

Despite many attempts over the years to close it down, Hell's Half Acre—Fort Worth's notorious red light district—managed to survive (at least in terms of the buildings) until thirteen city blocks were demolished beginning in the summer of 1965 to make way for the Tarrant County Convention Center. At the time, it was the biggest wrecking job in Texas, and a sizeable portion of Fort Worth's smaller turn-of-the-century commercial buildings were turned into dust. One small portion of the Acre lying south of the convention center—seen in the historic photograph—remained for a few years until construction began on the Fort Worth Water Gardens. Today, all that is left of the old Hell's Half Acre are tall tales. The Fort Worth/Tarrant County Convention Center, as it is now called, is currently undergoing renovation to provide facilities more suited to the needs of today's conventioneers.

Central Fire Station and the South Side from the 10th floor of the Medical Arts Building
1947

Overlooking Burnett Park on the western edge of the central business district, the eighteen-story Medical Arts Building stood away from other downtown skyscrapers and afforded spectacular views of Fort Worth to the south and west. The historic photograph looks southwest over the Central Fire Station No. 2 and Fire Alarm Signal Station towards Harris Methodist Hospital in the distance. The southern end of downtown with its mix of residential and commercial structures appears densely developed. In contrast, the contemporary photograph has a much more open feel because the freeway has replaced the buildings in the middle ground of the historic photograph. The Harris Hospital complex, in the distance—so open in the historic photograph—looks like the only densely developed portion of the contemporary image.

63

CHAPTER TWO

South Side

Edward T. Bergin Home, southeast corner of Henderson and El Paso
circa 1900

Edward T. Bergin and his father, John A. Bergin, operated the Fort Worth Marble and Granite Works near the courthouse square during the late nineteenth century. The family lived a few blocks away. After his father died in the mid-1890s, Edward built this charming shingled manse on the southeast corner of Henderson and El Paso streets at what would have been the extreme southern edge of the central business district. The area was then overwhelmingly residential despite its proximity to the Texas & Pacific Railway. The house was demolished about 1930 after serving as a rental property for several years. The land was vacant until 1938 when the Moderne style Dr Pepper Bottling Company plant, designed by noted architect Hubert Hammond Crane, was erected on the site. Today, the Dr Pepper building stands as a Fort Worth landmark in its own right.

Elizabeth Boulevard Gates, looking west from College Avenue
July 1912

Historic photograph courtesy Ryan Mortgage & Title

Elizabeth Boulevard was the focal point of developer John C. Ryan's restricted subdivision, Ryan Place. Inspired by the principles of the City Beautiful Movement, which held that the quality of city life could be improved through good urban design, Ryan laid out a broad boulevard with flanking trees, marble street curb signs, and two pair of massive stone entrance gates. These characteristics, he felt, would contribute to the livability and exclusive character of the neighborhood. The gates welcomed visitors and residents alike until 1958, when the main sections at both the east and west ends of the street were demolished because some believed them to be a traffic hazard. A Candlelight Christmas in Ryan Place raised funds to rebuild the western gates, located where Elizabeth intersects Eighth Avenue, in 1990, but the main section of the gates at the eastern end of Elizabeth, where it intersects College Avenue, have not been reconstructed.

69

West Broadway Avenue in the rain
1911-1912

West Broadway Avenue just east of Jennings was home to several "suburban" churches at the turn of the twentieth century. Residential development had only recently crossed the Texas & Pacific Railway tracks and moved south of the original town boundaries, bringing with it churches and other neighborhood institutions. The two churches pictured in the historic photograph are the new Broadway Baptist Church on the left and Broadway Presbyterian Church, with the steeply peaked roof, on the right. The previous buildings housing both congregations had been destroyed in a fire that ravaged the South Side on April 6, 1909. Temple Beth El, the only religious structure in the contemporary photograph, was completed in 1920 and had not been built when the first photograph was made. Broadway Baptist built a new sanctuary on the south side of Broadway between 1949 and 1952, but it still owns the lot where the 1910 church building once stood.

Forest Park Gates
circa 1920-1925

Fort Worth bought 74.73 acres of land to begin Forest Park in 1909 on the recommendation of park planner George Kessler. Reports called it a "wild and worthless area," but the addition of more acreage, the zoo, a swimming pool, and playing fields made Forest Park one of the city's most important recreation areas by the mid-1930s. These magnificent rubble stone gates were erected in 1917-1918 to mark the main entrance to Forest Park from Forest Park Boulevard. At that time, University Boulevard had not been extended south, so visitors entered the park via a landscaped drive off of Forest Park Boulevard that cut through a residential area. Land for the drive was donated by area landowner Samantha Sisk. The gates, designed by architect John Pollard, represent one of the city's early efforts to beautify its recreational facilities. Berkeley Place Association, representing the neighborhood located east of the park across Forest Park Boulevard, restored the gates in 1980.

73

Forest Park on a Sunday Afternoon
circa early 1930s

Historic photograph courtesy Fort Worth Public Library

Until the recent rapid expansion of the Fort Worth Zoo, the roadway through Forest Park was a narrow, two-lane affair that felt more like a rural path than a city street. Today, drivers out for a Sunday tour still encounter one landmark, the Forest Park Apartments constructed in 1927 and the most substantial "skyscraper" outside the central business district, as they climb the hill coming out of the park.

Company No. 5
firefighters on truck
circa 1910

Historic photograph courtesy Special Collections, University of Texas at Arlington Libraries

Company No. 5 has had an important role in the development of several Fort Worth Fire Department traditions. In 1903 or 1904, members of the W. B. Tucker Hose Company No. 5 represented Fort Worth in a skills contest at the State Fair of Texas. The wagon they planned to use badly needed a paint job, and the men of the company donated the money after the city council refused to appropriate funds. The painter, who received no instructions other than to "make it pretty," painted the wagon white with gold leaf and stripes. Company No. 5 won the State Fair competition, and since that time all Fort Worth fire trucks have been painted white in their honor. Station No. 5 was located at 501 Bryan Avenue when the historic photograph was taken and today is at 1000 Evans Avenue. In late 1909, the city purchased a new American La France combination chemical and hose wagon for $4,900 and placed it at Station No. 5. In this historic photograph Captain Marcellus Jameson, Lieutenant C. M. Ferguson, driver John D. Jones, and linemen Harry Bell and James Shea man the wagon. The truck was renovated several times and used to fight fires until the late 1940s, when it was probably the oldest piece of firefighting equipment in service anywhere in the United States. Contemporary firefighters are, Frank Becerra, Rick Jones, Scott Streator, and Lieutenant Todd Bagby.

Fairmount Avenue, looking north
circa 1915-1920

The Fairmount neighborhood is one of Fort Worth's oldest intact residential areas. It began to develop about 1905, after streetcar lines and city services were extended south from Pennsylvania Avenue. In a time when few families owned a car, it was essential either to be located within walking distance of work and shopping or to have access to public transportation. Filled with charming bungalows and four-squares, Fairmount was a solid middle-class neighborhood for two generations. Fairmount was listed on the National Register of Historic Places in 1990 as part of the Fairmount/Southside Historic District for its large and remarkably intact collection of early twentieth-century residential structures. Conditions in the neighborhood had declined following World War II when many of the original families died or moved, but the National Register listing has spurred revitalization. Today, with many of the bungalows lovingly restored, the 2100 block of Fairmount Avenue looks much as it did when first developed.

Historic photograph courtesy *Fort Worth Star-Telegram*

8th Ward (DeZavala) School playground
April 1912

A school serving elementary school age children of Fort Worth's South Side has stood on this site since 1905, and children have played on its grounds for as long. The school, which served students in the section of town called the 8th Ward, had the largest enrollment of any Fort Worth elementary school during the early years of the twentieth century. Located at 1419 College Avenue, the school was named to honor Lorenzo DeZavala, a hero of the Texas Revolution and the first vice-president of the Republic of Texas. The current "old" building is not present in the historic photograph, as it was constructed as an addition in 1914 two years after the playground image was taken. The 1905 section of the building was demolished in 1957-1958 when the current "modern" addition was constructed.

Texas Christian
University
1913

Fort Worth encouraged Texas Christian University to relocate here by offering fifty acres of land and $200,000 after a 1910 fire destroyed the school's main building in Waco. On opening day at the Fort Worth campus, September 16, 1911, three buildings—Goode Hall, The Main or Administration Building, and Jarvis Hall—had been completed. Goode Hall served as a men's dormitory, and Jarvis Hall housed female students. All three structures were yellow brick, Classical Revival buildings that gave the campus a dignified air, even if the landscaping was so severe as to be nonexistent. TCU was outside the Fort Worth city limits when it first opened, and housing development in the area was sparse despite the fact that the school sold residential lots to raise funds. Over the years, both the TCU campus and the neighborhoods surrounding it have aged gracefully. Many buildings are still built in a classical style, and trees shade the walkways that link the campus. Of the three original buildings, two—the Administration Building, now called Reed Hall, and Jarvis Hall—still stand, although they have been altered. Jarvis Hall still serves as a women's dormitory, and the school proudly notes that its residents have the highest grade point average of any dorm on campus.

Forest Park Boulevard, looking south from the 3100 block of Berry
December 1937

Historic photograph courtesy Special Collections, University of Texas at Arlington Libraries

Forest Park Boulevard was not paved south of Berry during the 1930s, and the *Fort Worth Star-Telegram* photographed the muddy scene as part of a series about the condition of local streets. In a caption that accompanied this photograph, the *Star-Telegram* noted that, "Drivers have nothing but a slip and a slide when they come to this point."

Hemphill Street at Magnolia Avenue
May 12, 1942

Historic photograph courtesy Special Collections, University of Texas at Arlington Libraries

Hemphill Street was widened to provide better access to the Federal Depot during World War II. The historic photo was taken to celebrate completion of the northern section of the widening project. With the exception of the signage, the traffic light, and the automobiles, the scene appears today much as it did sixty years ago. The Paris Coffee Shop, which was in business at a nearby location when the historic photograph was taken, remains a neighborhood fixture.

East-West Freeway (Interstate 30) looking east from Forest Park Boulevard
1952

Fort Worth began planning for a freeway system almost immediately after World War II ended. Two proposed expressways, the East-West and the North-South, were the main items on the street improvement bond election held on October 2, 1945. The initial section of the proposed East-West Freeway extended east from Camp Bowie Boulevard along Rosedale Street to Summit Avenue and then ran parallel to the Texas & Pacific Railway tracks to Cherry Street. At that point, it was to follow Lancaster Avenue to Boaz and then move northward one block and continue east to Virginia. Construction of the section from Montgomery Street to Summit Avenue was completed by October 1951. The historic photograph showing the section of freeway between Forest Park Boulevard and Summit Avenue was taken shortly afterwards. Current traffic conditions make it impossible to duplicate the historic photograph safely, so the contemporary image was shot from a point further west. The Westchester House retirement center on the right edge is the only major landmark visible in both photographs. The Medical Arts Building, barely peeking above the trees on the left edge of the historic photograph, has been replaced by the much taller One Burnett Plaza, and both Mrs. Baird's Bakery and the Summit Avenue Overpass have been demolished as part of the Interstate 30 reconstruction project.

89

Fort Worth Children's Hospital 2400 Winton Terrace West
circa 1957-1958

The Fort Worth Free Baby Hospital opened March 13, 1918, on Winton Terrace in the Park Hill Addition. Fairmount Land Company donated the lot, and most of the labor and construction materials were also donated. Sanguinet and Staats designed a one-story building, which was enlarged in 1923, when the name was changed to Fort Worth Children's Hospital. A community labor of love, the hospital provided free medical care for children who could not otherwise afford treatment. This photo was taken shortly before the hospital abandoned this facility and began constructing a new hospital at 1400 Cooper, adjacent to Harris Hospital. Fort Worth Children's Hospital merged with Cook Children's Medical Center in 1985 and built a new facility known as Cook-Fort Worth Children's Medical Center. Today, the house that replaced the hospital building is owned by a pediatrician who practices at Cook-Fort Worth Children's Medical Center.

Strip shopping center at 5320-5358 Wedgmont Circle
1957

Historic photograph courtesy Larry Schuessler

This Wedgwood-area strip shopping center is characteristic of post-war development that moved shops out of the central business district to the suburbs where people were living. The small stores were designed to be accessed by automobile, and the parking lot is almost more prominent than the building. Today, although the names of the stores have changed, the center is still home to the same types of businesses—convenience store, barber, and cleaners—that it housed originally.

North Side

Swift & Co.
meatpacking plant
from the
Livestock Exchange
Building roof
c. 1902-1910

Construction of the Armour and Swift meatpacking plants in 1902 gave Fort Worth its most significant economic boost since the arrival of the railroad in 1876. The historic view, taken from the roof of the Livestock Exchange Building, shows the hog and sheep pens before they were modernized in 1911, some of the livestock pens surrounding the Livestock Exchange, and the Swift & Co. operations in the distance. Symbolically, the Livestock Exchange Building was at the heart of stockyards operations as it was the headquarters from which livestock sales were made. Today, the handsome tile-roofed building presides over a successful district of a different sort, where the romance of the western livestock industry is celebrated and entertainment—at Stockyards Station, the Tarantula Railroad, the North Side Coliseum, and the Old Spaghetti Warehouse—is the primary commodity.

Fire Station #12
2410 Prospect
1910

Historic photograph courtesy Special Collections, University of Texas at Arlington Libraries

After the City of Fort Worth annexed North Fort Worth in 1909, it needed to provide city services for the residents. This fire station, located on a hill in a residential neighborhood overlooking the stockyards, was one of several virtually identical buildings designed by Fort Worth's premiere architectural firm, Sanguinet and Staats, and constructed around the city about this time. Firefighters moved into the new station on September 19, 1910. Today, the small wood-frame houses the station once protected are still there, but the station is now used as a day-care facility.

Googins Commercial Block
1539 North Main
& 101 Northwest
Twentieth streets
circa 1913

Historic photograph courtesy Special Collections, University of Texas at Arlington Libraries

Joseph B. Googins, developer and president of the North Fort Worth Townsite Company, built this prominent north side landmark about 1911, two years after North Fort Worth was annexed by the City of Fort Worth. The success of the Armour and Swift meatpacking plants drew many new workers and residents to North Fort Worth and created a need for housing and consumer services. Googins sited the building on a prominent corner at the intersection of North Main and Northwest Twentieth streets, outside the stockyards district but at the heart of the community. The building housed a drug store, barbershop, auto supply store, and millinery on the main floor and apartments upstairs. Today, both the retail spaces on the ground floor and the upstairs apartments are vacant.

Gates at Pioneers Rest Cemetery

Historic photograph courtesy Fort Worth Public Library

Pioneers Rest, Fort Worth's oldest burying ground, was established in 1850 when the military post—also known as Fort Worth—was active. When two of Commander Major Ripley Arnold's children died, Dr. Adolphus Gouhenant allowed them to be buried on his land. Baldwin L. Samuel gave three additional acres of land for the cemetery in 1871. Among the notable pioneers buried here are Ripley Arnold; Ephraim M. Daggett, called the Father of Fort Worth; and Tarrant County's namesake, General Edward H. Tarrant. While the fort was located on the bluff overlooking the Trinity River, in the general vicinity of today's Criminal Justice Building at 200 West Belknap Street, the cemetery was sited several blocks away from the fort along Samuels Avenue. Today, except for the growth of surrounding trees, the cemetery looks much the same as it did in the early years of the twentieth century.

Devastation caused by the Marine Creek flood
1942

Historic photograph courtesy Dalton Hoffman

The water that surged down Marine Creek in the early morning hours of April 19, 1942, came close to destroying the stockyards area. Heavy rains had swollen the Trinity River, and Marine Creek became a conduit for the torrent of raging water. Two tides of floodwaters—the first about 2:00 A.M. and the second three hours later—sent some smaller stockyards area buildings floating downstream and heavily damaged many others. Losses were estimated at $1.5 million. Debris carried by the floodwaters stacked up when it met resistance, such as the supporting walls of the culverts that allowed Marine Creek to flow under Exchange Avenue. Visitors who today stroll along the Marine Creek walkway can see this view of the back of the buildings along the south side of Exchange Avenue looking much as they did in 1942. The creek channel has, however, been engineered for flood control and landscaped so that Marine Creek now provides a pleasant addition to the stockyards landscape.

North Side High School Yell Leaders
1943

Historic photograph courtesy Quentin McGown, IV

Like football, cheerleading is a beloved activity in Texas. North Side High School opened in the fall of 1937 to educate the children of stockyard and packing plant workers. The historic photograph, taken in 1943, shows the squad with megaphones emblazoned with the names of North Side businesses. From left to right are Betty Lou White, Billy Burklow, Jimmy Garrison, Evelyn Riscky, Betty Jo Renner, Jo Dee Long, Bobby Robinson, and Bill Smith. Compared with the athletic stance of the current North Side High School cheerleading squad, they appear to be dressed for a more sedate church or school event rather than a vigorous workout. Yet, the photographs of both squads capture the sense of pride they feel as school representatives. Contemporary cheerleaders are Eduardo Chiapa, Mirella Peralta, Beth Hayes, Kim Avila, Alicia Benson (captain), Shaunte Zubiate, Adetola Adeyeye, Christina Raga, Victoria Barabas, Melissa Loyola, Maureen Toledo, John Paul Tovar.

CHAPTER FOUR

East Side

Glen Garden
Country Club
1922

Historic photograph courtesy Dalton Hoffman

Located in southeast Fort Worth on a hill overlooking the city, Glen Garden Country Club was chartered in 1912, making it the second oldest club in town, just slightly younger than Rivercrest. Glen Garden has always been popular for golf, and golfing greats such as Byron Nelson and Ben Hogan started their careers here as caddies. The Craftsman-style clubhouse, shown in the historic photograph, was built in 1914 but extensively remodeled in the 1950s. The 1922 photograph shows employees of the Washer Brothers department store enjoying a picnic in front of the clubhouse. In 2000, the club built a new clubhouse on the lawn in front of the old one, so today golfers and carts take the place of picnickers.

East Lancaster Avenue Parkway under Construction
February 7, 1938

Historic photograph courtesy Special Collections, University of Texas at Arlington Libraries

The historic photograph was taken for a *Fort Worth Star-Telegram* article documenting construction of the East Lancaster Avenue Parkway. The old road, with commercial structures flanking it, is on the right, and construction to build a new median and roadway can be seen to the left. Both views were taken on Lancaster just west of Beach Street looking towards downtown from a high point in the road. Although many of the buildings along Lancaster have changed, the graceful curve of the parkway and the eye-catching view of the downtown skyline still remain. The Sinclair service station building is still there, too, although it has been significantly altered.

I. M. Terrell
School Library
circa late 1930s

Historic photograph courtesy Tarrant County Black Historical and Genealogical Society

I.M. Terrell is a school reborn. As Fort Worth's segregated high school for area African-American students, Terrell operated out of a smaller building nearby from 1921 to 1938 and was housed in this bluff-top facility on East Eighteenth Street between 1938 and 1973. Between 1955-1956 and 1973, a fourteen-room addition also allowed the facility to serve junior high school students. The historic library photograph was probably taken in the East Eighteenth Street facility shortly after the building opened. Many of Fort Worth's African-American leaders attended Terrell, and the school is remembered fondly as a place that nurtured academic achievement for minority students at a time when segregation severely limited their business and social options. Terrell served as a continuing education center for several years after the high school closed and then was vacant. Recent revitalization in Fort Worth's central business district and surrounding neighborhoods led to the need for additional school facilities, and in the fall of 1998 the renovated building was reopened as an elementary school. The computers and other library resources available to today's diverse student body are a reminder of how much change has occurred in the past sixty years.

Fourth Street
Underpass
circa 1930

Historic photograph courtesy *Fort Worth Star-Telegram*

Fourth Street was historically a main travel artery between downtown Fort Worth and Riverside. This underpass, replacing one without a storm sewer that was erected in 1910, allowed traffic to move beneath the Rock Island Railway tracks.

116

*East Rosedale Street
looking east
towards Cobb Park*
July 19, 1936

During the early 1930s, Rosedale consisted of many short segments that were not connected, making cross-town travel difficult. This construction project extended East Rosedale to Sycamore Creek at the western edge of Cobb Park. In the historic photograph, workers are laying brick on a concrete base. Although it provided a bumpy ride by today's standards, brick was a favored paving material because it was durable and the spaces between the bricks allowed them to move as the weather changed without creating potholes. Laying brick streets was also labor intensive, providing jobs for men who were unemployed during the Depression. Today, those brick pavers are hidden beneath a coating of asphalt and Highway 287 obscures the view of the Polytechnic Heights neighborhood to the east.

119

East Rosedale Street looking east from Nashville Avenue
1937

This section of East Rosedale marks the approach to Texas Wesleyan University. The Ashburn Ice Cream Company Building at 3012-14 East Rosedale, identified by the ice cream cone-shaped sign at the center right of the historic photograph, operated at this location through the late 1980s. Nashville intersects Rosedale at an angle, and the parallel sets of curving streetcar tracks follow the road. During the 1930s, this section of Rosedale was a densely developed thoroughfare with a wide variety of shops and services. Today, a number of the buildings are vacant or have been demolished—leaving a gap-toothed arrangement of boarded up storefronts and parking lots interspersed with small businesses. Stability in a commercial neighborhood is established with a series of viable businesses operating near each other, and Rosedale would benefit from the strength that comes from having such neighbors.

121

Northern Texas Traction Company Car Barns
circa 1920s

Historic photograph courtesy Dalton Hoffman

Sometimes the use of a place has a logical continuity even though it may not be obvious to the casual viewer. The Northern Texas Traction Company ran the Fort Worth-Dallas Interurban and several local streetcar routes during the first decades of the twentieth century. During the 1930s, when streetcars gave way to buses, the area used to store and repair the cars shown in this historic photograph became a bus barn—and is today home to "The T," the Fort Worth Transportation Authority's administrative offices, bus barns, and maintenance facilities.

Entrance to Fort Worth (Highway 80 at eastern city limits looking west)
January 1942

Arthur Rothstein took a series of photographs in the Fort Worth-Dallas area for the Farm Security Administration/Office of War Information, a Depression-era relief project. Most of his images in Fort Worth were of aircraft construction at the bomber plant or aviation training at Meacham Field, but he also made several pictures along the main Fort Worth-to-Dallas highway. This location marks Fort Worth's eastern city limits in 1942, and the historic photograph has a distinctively rural feeling, while the contemporary image shows the toll of time on our urban infrastructure. What a difference sixty years makes.

Martin Luther King, Jr., Day Parade
1975

Historic photograph courtesy Tarrant County Black Historical and Genealogical Society

Celebrations commemorating the life of civil rights leader Martin Luther King, Jr., began shortly after he was assassinated in 1968. Fort Worth Mayor R. M. "Sharky" Stovall proclaimed the city's first Martin Luther King Day in 1970, and the first parade was probably held in 1972. The parade shown in the historic photograph took place in the heart of the African-American business district on Evans Avenue in 1975. In later years, as the celebration of King's birthday was more widely embraced, the parade location was moved to the central business district.

127

West Side

Lake Como
circa 1907-1917

Historic photograph courtesy Special Collections, University of Texas at Arlington Libraries

Constructed to provide cooling for the Arlington Heights streetcar electric generating plant, Lake Como was named after the famous Swiss resort. The lake and adjacent pavilion quickly became a favorite Fort Worth amusement place even though it was a twenty-minute streetcar ride from downtown. Guests got off on the east side of the lake and walked across the white bridge connecting the streetcar stop with the pavilion. Boating and water sports were popular activities, but guests also attended symphony and ragtime concerts. Lake Como closed just before World War I according to a 1924 *Fort Worth Press* article, "its business smashed by the automobiles, Lake Worth and Gloria Swanson." Troops stationed at Camp Bowie used Lake Como for boating practice during World War I since the lake was conveniently located at the western edge of the camp. Shortly after the war, residential development around the lake began for African-Americans who worked as domestics in Arlington Heights homes, and the name Como was applied to the neighborhood as well as the lake. In late 1952, businessman Amon G. Carter donated the lake and surrounding acreage to the City of Fort Worth for a "Negro Park," and the lake—which by that time was overgrown with cattails—was cleaned and equipped for park use.

Camp Bowie Boulevard looking west
1927

Camp Bowie Boulevard was originally known as Arlington Heights Boulevard because it connected Fort Worth with its first subdivision three miles to the west. In 1890, when they platted the development, the developers also built a streetcar line in the median to provide transportation for Arlington Heights residents and Fort Worth citizens who came to enjoy outdoor activities at Lake Como. By 1927, when the historic photograph was taken for a Northern Texas Traction Company report, the street had been renamed for the World War I army camp, Arlington Heights was full of new bungalows, and the amusements at Lake Como were shuttered. Streetcar service along this route ended in 1936 when buses were deemed a more efficient way to transport visitors to Fort Worth's Frontier Centennial celebration. Today, the street still retains its neighborhood appeal thanks in part to the low-rise commercial buildings flanking both sides of the parkway, the preservation of historic brick paving, and landmark buildings like the 1922 Arlington Heights Masonic Lodge that still sits, on an angle, on its triangular corner lot.

Historic photograph courtesy Fort Worth Public Library

132

133

*Trinity Park
entrance gate on
West Seventh Street*
circa 1910

The land comprising the northern portion of Trinity Park along the Trinity River was used informally as a picnic ground before the city began to purchase the property from owner K. M. Van Zandt in 1892. Between 1892 and 1928, the city purchased 217 acres in eight parcels, forming Fort Worth's first public park, but few improvements were made. In 1907, a group of civic-minded women raised funds to build the park gateway shown in this historic photograph. Their efforts coincided with the hiring of noted city planner George Kessler, who developed the first park plan for Fort Worth, and the establishment of a Board of Park Commissioners in 1909. The Trinity Park Shelter that defines the northern section of the park today was constructed in 1935-1937 along with trails, lagoons, and fountains as part of a Public Works Administration Depression-era relief project.

Trinity River/City Park
circa 1906-1909

During the 1880s, Fort Worth's first water system drew from the Trinity, and even now a portion of the city's water supply comes from lakes formed by dams on the river. City Park, later part of Trinity Park, was created in 1892 from land adjacent to the Trinity that was part of a tract purchased to build the Holly Water Plant. The Holly Plant drew some of the water it supplied to city residents from the Trinity, and the concrete structure in these photographs and the low dam were probably part of the system that facilitated pumping water from the river. The presence of the utilitarian concrete structure in a scenic park image speaks to the significant role that water played in the development of Fort Worth. Even though the Trinity River has not proven to be commercially navigable, it is significant not only for the water it provides but for the way in which it has shaped the city. Periodic flooding once dictated where facilities and neighborhoods would be built, and early park planner George Kessler wisely centered the city's park system on the river. Today, the significance of this odd chunk of concrete is lost to most people, but it is a tangible reminder of the ways in which the city is linked with the Trinity River.

West Lancaster Avenue, looking east towards downtown
1939

The area known today as the Cultural District is located on land purchased in the early 1870s by pioneer Fort Worth businessman and civic leader K. M. Van Zandt. During the 1930s, when Amon Carter was looking for a site for the Fort Worth Frontier Centennial, Van Zandt's heirs sold a 138-acre tract to the City of Fort Worth to house the centennial festivities. The historic photograph, taken three years after the centennial from a rise near the intersection of Montgomery and Lancaster, shows West Lancaster as it cut through the centennial grounds, sloping towards the Trinity River and downtown. The hilltop was reportedly one of Carter's favorite views of downtown, and he chose it as the site for the Amon Carter Museum, under construction behind the plywood fence on the left in the contemporary photograph. Today, the many trees obscure the view of downtown from Lancaster, but the handsome historic streetlights remain.

Stock Show Midway from the Ferris Wheel
March 1947

Historic photograph courtesy Fort Worth Public Library

After a brief hiatus during the Second World War, the Southwest Exposition and Fat Stock Show (the word "fat" was dropped from the show's name in 1989) moved from the North Side to the Will Rogers Complex in 1944. The move provided not only more parking and exhibit space but gave the Midway ride and entertainment area room to expand as well. Surprisingly, the feel of the Midway, with its enticements seems to have changed little in the past fifty or so years. It is still a place to fork over just a bit too much money and forget the cares of the day as you shoot, spin, and guzzle with abandon.

141

Consolidated Vultee
Aircraft Corporation
assembly line
circa 1944

The "bomber plant's" mile-long assembly line in White Settlement turned out 120 B-24s per month at peak production, and the seemingly endless row of planes demonstrated the plant's crucial role in both national defense during the Second World War and the Fort Worth economy. Production practices have changed dramatically over the years, and today the assembly line has a completely different feel with fewer planes assembled in a modular fashion.

Historic photograph courtesy Lockheed Martin

142

Automobile Row on West Seventh Street, looking east towards downtown
circa 1938-1939

Historic photograph courtesy Fort Worth Public Library

During the 1930s and 1940s, the section of West Seventh Street between Henderson and Penn streets was known as Automobile Row. A variety of services from new car dealers to repair shops lined both sides of the street. Today most of the auto-related businesses have moved to the outskirts of town. They have been replaced by vacant lots and, more recently, new downtown housing. One vintage automobile building on the north side of Seventh Street serves as a reference point for both the historic and contemporary photographs. It originally housed the city's Packard dealership but by the mid-1930s was home to H. B. Ransom's Fort Worth Motors, Inc., which sold Chrysler and Plymouth automobiles. Today it is used for retail and offices. A few automobile repair facilities remain in the vicinity, but overall, this area has seen substantial change since dealerships began to move away in the 1950s and 1960s.

Botanic Garden-Rose Garden and Terraces
circa 1940s

Historic photograph courtesy Quentin McGown, IV

Long a popular spot for weddings and Mother's Day outings, the rose ramp at the Botanic Garden was designed by landscape architect S. Herbert Hare and built in 1933-1934 with loan funds provided by the Reconstruction Finance Corporation. It was the first federal relief project undertaken in Fort Worth and remains one of the city's most beloved Depression-era endeavors. The pond or lagoon at the foot of the terraces was originally fed by Rock Springs, which gave its name to the park before the Rose Garden was constructed. When the freeway just south of the garden was being constructed in the early 1950s, the natural spring dried up, and water is now pumped in from the Trinity River.

Lake Worth (Nine-Mile) Bridge
circa 1920

Historic photograph courtesy Larry Schuessler

The name Nine-Mile Bridge came from the fact that the bridges at this site crossed Lake Worth nine miles out of Fort Worth. Lake Worth was completed in 1914 by damming the West Fork of the Trinity River to provide a water supply for Fort Worth and a municipal recreational center. The facility along the shoreline in the historic photograph is the bathhouse that served the bathing beach. A casino was built on the south side of the bridge in 1927, and a bridge with concrete railings replaced this one in 1929. That bridge was demolished in 1987, but the current bridge is still known as Nine-Mile Bridge.

Highway 183 and
Roberts Cut-off
1953

Although located in River Oaks, this site has fond memories for many Fort Worth families because it marks the turnoff to the YMCA's Camp Carter. Established in 1950, Camp Carter afforded generations of baby boomers the opportunity to get away from city life and spend the summer playing by the shores of Lake Worth. Remarkably, the character of this intersection has changed very little over the years. It still has the feel of a rural crossroads.

Lake Worth from Inspiration Point
circa 1940

Historic photograph courtesy Quentin McGown, IV

Inspiration Point is located in Marion Sansom Park on a promontory overlooking Lake Worth. The view, perhaps the source of the site's name, offers a dramatic panorama of the lake, dam, and fish hatchery. Inspiration Point is one of a number of park facilities constructed around Lake Worth as part of Depression-era work relief projects and features a charming rock shelter house. It was a great place to watch fighter jets take off and land from Carswell Air Force Base, but many Fort Worth baby boomers and prime timers will remember Inspiration Point in the words of a *Fort Worth Star-Telegram* writer as, "the city's most famous parking lot."

Index